Books by Richard Howard

Poetry

MISGIVINGS *1979*

FELLOW FEELINGS *1976*

TWO-PART INVENTIONS *1974*

FINDINGS *1971*

UNTITLED SUBJECTS *1969*

THE DAMAGES *1967*

QUANTITIES *1962*

Criticism

ALONE WITH AMERICA *1969*

PREFERENCES *1974*

Misgivings

MISGIVINGS

Poems by *Richard Howard*

New York *Atheneum* 1979

The poems have been previously published as follows:

TO THE PAINTERS *in the catalogue,* AMERICA 1976, *for a Bicentennial Exhibition sponsored by the United States Department of the Interior*
STITCHING IN TIME *in Georgia Review*
THEBAIS *in The New Yorker*
A COMMISSION *in The New Republic*
HOMAGE TO NADAR:
    Charles Garnier in Poetry
    Sarah Bernhardt in Christopher Street
    Victor Hugo in The New Leader
    Honoré Daumier in Ploughshares
    Jacques Offenbach in October
    Gioachino Rossini in October
    Richard Wagner in October
    Charles Baudelaire in The Nation
    Edmond and Jules De Goncourt in Christopher Street
    Gustave Doré in Christopher Street
    Théophile Gautier in Christopher Street
    George Sand in The Nation
    Nadar in Antaeus
DOMESTICITIES *in Christopher Street*
ANOTHER INVITATION *in The New Yorker*
CODES *in The Georgia Review*
WITH THE REMOVER TO REMOVE *in The Georgia Review*
WITH A POTPOURRI FROM DOWN UNDER *in The Paris Review*

for David Osborne

> *I woke. You were not there. But as I dressed*
> *Anxiety turned to shame, feeling my dreams*
> *Intended one rebuke. For had not each*
> *In its own way tried to teach*
> *My will to love you that it cannot be,*
> *As I think, of such consequence to want*
> *What anyone is given, if they want?*
>
> A U D E N , *The Lesson*

I

I I *Homage to Nadar*

I I I

(I)

To the Painters

On the United States, Considered as a Landscape

Not a building, this earth, not a cage,
    these waters: the country is
a body, to be treated so: when
    the weather is mild, think
of the past, when the weather is mean,
    think of the future. Men do
thus, and evolve a metropolis
    from litter: leaves, straw, floating
bottles and boxes, a mainland which,
    like anything else, cannot
be made all at once to drop its rags,
    suddenly to stand naked,
fully disclosed. Time—it has taken
    time to collect in wide pools
even the beginnings, skeleton
    and cartilege, arteries
and bladder: if our Sublime cannot
    rise above such things as beer
cans and plastic picnic forks, it is
    not all we say, it cannot
really be the God in which we trust.

Who creates by transforming, until
    we know the joy of having
ourselves—the Master of Qualified
    Assertion puts it this way—
having ourselves been created by
    whatever has been endured
and mastered in the past: agreement
    with reality is not

      necessarily agreeable,
          but there may be in the world
    around us things (is a beach a thing?
          a river between red bluffs?)
    which solace as well as any ruin
          could, or the funeral rites
of Phocion, say, in the distance . . .
          Maybe there is no difference,
among us, between the God and his
          Temple—that would be success,
the undefiled American thing
          our Master of Dogmatic
Doubt calls the bravery to be new.

We have another Master, hear him—
          he is neither qualified
nor dogmatic, he is a man there,
          on the scene: "A good day here,
amid the sand and salt, a steady
          breeze setting in from the sea,
the sun shining, the sedge odor, noise
          of the surf, a mixture of
hissing and booming, the milk-white crests
          curling over. Leisurely
I bathed and had a naked ramble
          as of old on the warm gray
shore, my companions off in a boat
          in deeper water (I hailed
my friends with Jupiter's menaces
          against the gods, from Homer)."
Even Walt requires a god—requires
          Homer, Pope's Homer! to make
the moment more than facts that harass
          like flies, buzz but do not sing.
Have we said yet what we had to say?

Are we at home here, have we made this
    our place? Following the lines
between the States, a plane gave Gertrude
    Stein her vision, "made it right
that I had always been with cubism and
    everything that came after."
Straight lines ("compare them to the others,
    the ones that go all over,
nothing neat and clean like the maps of
    America") and Indian names
no one knows, only recognizes,
    Latin names who remembers?
Looking back we do not remember
    ourselves but the neighborhoods
we lived in and the things there we knew
    (is a marsh a thing? and what
the sun makes of western windows, pane
    after pane igniting?). How
much we belong to the past we learn
    only when we have labored
to survive and prevail without it.

Keeping up with the body, then, till
    it falls where it may, we know
what our exertions teach: everyone
    who makes something new does harm
to something old. Inside what we make,
    or what we have made, inside
our work is another work trying
    to get out. We help it out,
doing harm, for we are not at home
    in this literal climate,
terrain without metaphor, without
    reference to preference:
the leaves are too green and the rocks
    too red, the sea around us

    is a sea of silent blasphemies.
        It is all too new for us,
and somehow too old as well: we are
        not safe here, and we know it.
Our knowledge is our hope, as we look
        out the window and over
the cliff . . . We change and, ourselves changing,
        change what we see: this beloved,
defiled and continuing body.

Stitching in Time: Dorothy Ruddick

The only god whose name
we know: Mutation . . .

Remember that day on the beach, remember
    how we marvelled at the sea's design
        abandoned merely to chance—
unpredictable, inevitable, so
    we called it chance—that shining scarf of foam
        repeatedly wreathed on itself
in the long love-letters ocean writes to land?

Remember then the bonfire we found—burnt out,
    the ashes organized by their spent
        soul into the fire's design,
dying in whispers we were not meant to hear,
    till only the song was left, silent
        structure of the log that once
had shouted green as any limb in our woods?

And the clouds came on, faster it seemed for all
    the light they limited, until one
        kind of future was past: gone
in the altered pattern of a darkness asking
    no more than submission from the air—
        remember the clouds that afternoon,
racing each other to see which would fade first?

But earth faded first, remember? how the fields
    went out, or went up into darkness,
        clamoring above themselves
like a clumsy burglar leaving too many
    clues to a far from perfect crime: night
        never falls, night rises, and this—
this after all can happen only on earth.

Water and fire, air and the ground, losing and
        gaining at once—elements always
                simultaneously say
Yes and No—you have remembered! Here they are
        on the modest cloth, intricate
                obstinance of the insect
combining with the mystic's fixed ambition
        to declare, stitch by stitch, what cannot
                be abridged: *this has the ring's*
will in it, this joy, this renunciation
        of yourself, of whatever is not
                chosen. Between Arachne
who made too well and Penelope who unmade,
        you have gone about your daily task,
                the business of purgatory.
Ask the fact for the form: material things!

Thebais

*In the next small room we find Star-
nina's panel depicting the lives of
saintly hermits in a landscape
which shows the artist to have had
a highly developed understanding
of nature. Starnina (1354?–1403?)
remains, however, an enigmatic fig-
ure; Berenson does not mention
him, and the attempt to attribute
this picture to the young Uccello
was never convincing.*

GUIDE TO THE UFFIZI

for Cynthia Macdonald

There are, by my tally, just a hundred
of us here, monks living and dead, maybe
more—without a jeweler's loupe, who could tell?
nor am I sure the dead ones count, except
to suggest a symbolic enterprise
to the living (more about that later) . . .
We are all over the place, even up
in a tree, even down in the dragon's
mouth—look over there on the extreme right,
just beyond the white-walled village, see him?

your common or yellow-bellied dragon
waiting for one of us to wade across,
above the double bridge, where the water
thins to a more negotiable gold,
though why that dragon fails to negotiate
the stream in our direction I can't guess—
all the other animals are here, beasts
of burden, birds of prey, one dancing bear,

and there comes Brother Anselm from behind
the ragged hills, riding on a leopard!

I always said there was something showy
about Brother Anselm, he could never
be content like the rest of us to ward
off jackals, herd our long-horned antelope,
or discipline a fox which has just gnawed
through the neck of Father Eustace's hen—
do you see anyone else riding? No,
we walk, even on water, or else we are
transported, as by devils, through the air
to bleak caves with little more than a bell

and a basket to make our wants known. Wants!
We farm, we fish, and Brother Fred can bake
(if you call that baking). Once in a while
someone remembers us and sends real bread
from town—you might suppose those two in red
gowns were angels, up where George the novice
is reading to the new abbot (we read lots),
but they are merely rich ladies who hope
to have it both ways; every now and then
they stay the night, listening. Then we feast,

and that brings me—feasting does—to my point,
or at least to my line. Any depiction
of human life—and Lord knows, ours is that,
if "human" means warfare with what is not—
goes to show nothing exists by itself,
not even the eminent thunder rattling
St. Antony who has just wrapped St. Paul
(of Thebes, dead at 113)
in a yellow mantle he had himself
received from Athanasius, attended

by one of our reverent lions (rather
a desert specialty, that); not even,
between the pines, some intricate red roofs
which correspond to a red-silk binding
of the sermon read over a red silk bier
of our patriarch of earthly arcades
in the opposite corner; not even . . .
But it is hard for me to put you in
the picture over here: there have been no
enlargements made of the entire left half,

we must abide by a general sense of pink
and delicate architecture reproached
by certain precipices only, for
as the Preacher saith, better is the sight
of the eye than the wandering of desire.
And it *is* better, this unrequited
attachment of ours to things in general,
this long perspective we might call tragic
if we did not, like Starnina, call it
love: taken out of scale, taken close up,

it is holocaust. I say Starnina
"calls" it love, by which I mean he labors
to label what he shows, and thereby
calls it love, these coenobite practices
he discovers to us in little boats,
on large boulders, among lilac buildings,
for love is shown in violence, supreme
love in levity. Which joy, once a meager
publicity of pagans, is for this painter
the giant secret of his anchorites

whose world is an adventure, not a scheme,
and our differences from each other

an absolute sanctity. Nothing
exists by itself . . . Who is the man, anyway,
this Starnina of ours? One Gherardo
of Florence, who being nobler in blood
than in nature, by Vasari's account,
brought more harm on himself than on his friends
thereby; and more harm still would have brought
if he had not dwelt a long time in . . . Spain!

where he learned gentleness and courtesy,
so that on returning, those who bore him
hatred received him lovingly. Spain then,
or the desert behind Thebes—any place
of trial is inconceivable without
a semblance of self-exposure. And then
disappearance. Maybe we are not his
at all, because there was no Starnina . . .
Look! a man may vanish as God vanished,
by filling all things with created life.

Another Language

What would you say to Mr Tanaka under the following circumstances?
Give Mr Tanaka's reply to the preceding, wherever possible.

1 You have met him in the morning
2 You meet again in the same place that evening
3 You offer him a cigarette
4 He has just given you something
5 You have touched him
6 Something unpleasant has happened
7 You are leaving

I hope it stops raining soon
The clouds are purple over there
Can we share this pleasure
That is just what I want
How strange it feels
I cannot bear any more
Please forgive me

It is always wet this time of year
The dark comes sooner every day
Pain is easier to share
I will always try to satisfy your desires
What others have is foreign
Only a moment longer
I am sorry to lose you

A Commission

for the composer Dan Erkkila

Of course you will cut dead anything
    that savors of Richard Strauss
and the stews of MittelEuropa—
    already there has been far
too much fantastication and self-
    indulgence, too much brocade
of the Great-Gold-Curtain variety.
    Let us have no Big Scenes, no
revelations that come down (stage) to
    some diva uneasily
divested of every last sequin
    until there she lies, winded,
a stocky body in a body stocking . . .

No, getting her clothes off has nothing
    to do with the requirements;
your job is to make certain the girl
    has good reason to get dressed!
For months she has been running around
    the palace in no more than
a necklace, pestering the staff and
    embarrassing visitors
with her endless whining: "Watch me dance!
    Watch me dance!" Now you must make
an occasion for her to put on
    finery, robe after robe,
until she startles everyone, swagged

and swathed: the image of her mother!
    Not until the very end,

though, is the resemblance apparent—
    you have to devise something
(ten minutes is what I have in mind)
    austere: not only a holding
back from pleasure, but whose suspension
    will be a source of pleasure
in itself. Which is why I suggest
    you go back, or go sideways,
to the music of other cultures . . .
    our own has relied too much
on the passage of time, capitalized

on the lure of foreward movement. Now
    I want you to overcome
or disregard that sense of direction
    toward a final cadence.
A flute should do it, two minor drums
    and those brass finger-cymbals
the child stole from one of her mother's
    maids when the Romans arrived
and caused so much confusion at Court.
    And that's all—easy enough,
I'm sure, for a man of your resources
    (let these intentions be made
audible, not these calculations). . . .

Oh yes, one thing more. Just at the end
    I need a tremendous touch,
not so much loud as a contrast of
    loud and almost inaudible:
thanks to your work, you see, the gestures
    of taking on have *taken*,
that is the ritual your little set
    of variations (you did
have something of the sort in mind, no?)
    incarnates, so when Herod

has her strangled, it is for turning
    into Herodias, not
for that business with the head, about

which he couldn't care less. Compose me
    a cadence of last resort,
if I may say so, the finality
    we lack in Salome's dance
with its circular realizations—
    especially if we start
with no more than a sliding scale
    from the flute (hard to improve
on Strauss there, but you can find something
    even more inevitable,
even simpler). . . . The moon is red now
    and the stage is dark, except
for Salome, dead in her robes, that woman.

(I I)

HOMAGE TO NADAR

for Susan Sontag

To call our sight Vision
implies that, to us,
all objects are subjects.

*

What we have not named
or beheld as a symbol
escapes our notice.

*

The camera records
visual facts: i.e.,
all may be fictions.

A U D E N , *I Am Not a Camera*

Charles Garnier

If no one had heard of you, it was hardly
    your fault, more likely a foretaste
of the stubborn obscurity still to come—

    graduating with a Grand Prix,
you buggered away your hopes in Greece, begging
    permission from the puzzled Turks

to measure intervals between the pillars
    of Zeus Panhellenios, coy
yourself about the purpose but doggedly

    coloring the friezes faded
past recognition while Aegina lay ripe
    for the taking under your hands:

the boys, the nymph and her polychrome marbles
    were no preparation for fame,
nor a dozen water-colors "well-received"

    at the 1860 Salon . . .
Who was more astonished than yourself, next year,
    when *your* Opéra was chosen

from all their monumentalities? But if
    we have accepted everything
we have missed something—war. Until that came too,

    and your monster had to abide
thirteen years and a German occupation
    before it stood revealed—exposed—

to history and your doom: preposterous
       success and silence to the end,
which included your plans for the Casino

     at Monte Carlo and sculptures
commissioned from Doré and Sarah Bernhardt!
       Chance and Art, superior sports

between your wars and ours, diversions made you
       immortal, loved, and forgotten.
Your coat bulges below the Order of . . . what?

     and your hair is beyond disorder:
did they wear steel-wool wigs in the Paris of
       Napoléon III? You regard

what Nadar called the objective straight on, young
       still, and with the intrepid stare
of a very brave ram, cornered but not cowed.

Sarah Bernhardt

Often enough you were naked under the cloak
    in those days; gentlemen drank
and waited, murmuring deprecations

    till the cloak dropped and your arms
which would dishevel the world—those white serpents,
    Hugo called them—were exposed,

thin as your legs, thin and white, but rusted here,
    then here, the rest white and hard . . .
Not yet: you have not yet had success on the stage,

    and if you were a mother two
years back, Maurice never knew his father—
    did you? A nun, you wanted

to be a nun, and became a sculptor, one
    craning female torso sent
each year to the Salon, ardent clay ladies

    in postures of possession.
Mortal will is already your mode, undressed,
    uncombed, probably unwashed—

you are the child he wrote in French for, Oscar
    who understood your crying
need and overheard, just thirty years too late,

    the voice of Salome, pure
gold bangles on a tin wire pulled to breaking,
    and of course the wire did break.

Sarah Bernhardt

You seem to be regarding, on cue but still
    offstage, in the studio,
the resonant hells your talent sanctified

    for decades of unbelievers.
And taught your century its lesson, dying
    in *La Gloire*, your last *relâche*

attended by a house of fifty thousand:
    dazed Paris, unforgiving,
relented for your farewell tour of duty

    which was to doubt if either
the Heavenly City or that wan shade of it
    our dreams have perpetuated

can function, flourish, or even form unless
    it include its opposite,
unless in heaven there is hell. Divine Sarah.

Victor Hugo

The deathbed portrait

You made darkness your own secret and declared
    "no one keeps secrets better
than children." Yours kept theirs best of all, dying

    or delirious before you—
no: you were always mad, but always alive
    until this pious keepsake

showed you had no secrets left to keep, lying
    dead as Charles and François, mad
as Adèle, merely one more carcass in your

    century's series of clean
old men who look like God. Yet cover yourself
    with light as with a garment—

even your beard, still growing under eyes grown
    still, becomes a burning bush.
Yourself! Who troubles now to identify

    such remains, consequences
of a theory condemned, like every theory,
    to masterpieces or else

to oblivion—who finds you out today?
    Swinburne was your last zealot,
Gide regretted, and we—we doubt everything

    but the frenzied *aquarelles*
which prove real silence is the end of language,
    not just the stopping of it.

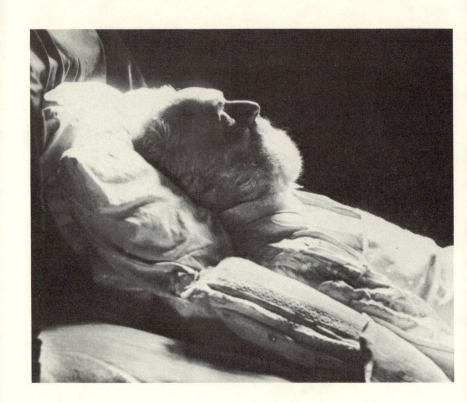

No darkness here, no secret save the impression
      of being a personage
who became extinct without ever having been

      a volcano . . . Your face is
Faust's but with the light of hell gone out of it,
      replaced by magnesium

and an embargo from heaven, Daumier said,
      because you insisted so
on calling God *cher maître*. Ancient of Days

      and innocent of days, take
this day our daily darkness for who you were,
      the chiaroscuro lesson

taken but never given: there is only
      one pleasure—that of being
alive. All the others are a misery.

Honoré Daumier

The absurd has its reasons which the reason
            absorbs: now the outlines throb
when you draw, and the decade of sight left you

        will leave you diligently
vulnerable to the long littleness of life,
        who revealed so little else—

for you humanity was definable
        broadly by its weaknesses
or narrowly as your crayon could encroach

        upon the printed province
of that other Honoré who found the fraud
        in your tiny lead sculptures:

"This man has a touch of Michelangelo
        in him trying to get out!"
You gaze into the future which is darkness

        gathering at the far end
of Nadar's studio, as if you understood
        that from now on you must force

the edges of things to fulfill their centers—
        to you it is apparent
that the first portrait was a skull. No wonder

        you can paint nothing, these days,
but Sancho and his Don, flesh and the mad bones
        coursing across a bright plain

which is hell with hope in it, the real hell.
Shadows are wanted; you work
by too much light to believe the visible—

we need to keep in the shade
of Something that is greater than what we see
and that we don't want to face

all the time. You will provide manner with fact
and let matter, thus obscured,
dispose of itself. What you have kept will earn

its keep, not theory but thirst,
one vision sustaining you twenty blind years:
it is a truth that all men

are tragic, even a sublime truth; it is
a truth equally sublime
that all men are comic. And you never lied.

Jacques Offenbach

Your great days are gone, great days are always gone,
        and only the clothes remain
to prove how rich you were and if German once

        or even Jewish, still French
by Imperial decree and the Emperor's
        own tailor. Yards of sable

cannot smother apprehensions—bankruptcy
        hovers like the next good tune,
and you strain your ears for that inspired stammer

        which precedes all melody . . .
Henceforth there will be no major breakthroughs but
        some marvellous backsliding:

the vogue has grown too vast for suave allusions
        to Verdi and Meyerbeer
—your magenta period—hence a skeleton

        in pince-nez and puce knit gloves
prepares one more time to rape the double-bass,
        a cantor's son from Cologne

now "the little Mozart of the Champs-Elysées"
        according to Rossini,
who should know. Your face is a cold rooster's, old

        cock fresh out of sunrises,
and you take off your pince-nez as carefully
        as if it were a dragon-

fly, breathing brimstone on the lenses. To the pure
     all things are rotten, and you
have made music so profligate it is no

     wonder more Germans would come
to Paris and suppress it with cannonballs.
     Whereupon the foam died down.

Not even the New World can indemnify
     Orpheus from your underworld;
miracles of wit and monsters of moral

     obtuseness sufflaminate
your hopes for *Hoffmann* (never heard) by one last
     succès d'animosité . . .

Genius balked only because you could not bear
     to be alone with talent:
the will says *free* and the world says *lost*.

Gioachino Rossini

How much you could have told me, Maestro, about
    wigs (who needs to know it all),
wearing here a sleek horsehair effrontery

    over frizzled white sideburns,
brazening the vast fraud past vanity *or* art,
    even wearing, sometimes, two,

one on top of the other—for warmth, you claimed,
    extinguishing cheeky stares
by a "speaking likeness," this hard look that says

    *I know I'm making a fool
of myself, but what else have I left?* Vale-
    tudinarianism

lasting twenty years has its lesson to teach:
    a man must begin to love
in order to avoid falling ill, as Freud

    subsequently reported.
Gift or giveaway, *success* and its sequel,
    silence, equally immense,

round off every corner of your countenance,
    and behind those lizard lids
the words *genius* and *failure* represent

    nothing really existing,
only a stage of understanding ourselves.
    Not that you breathed such words, for

breathing came hard—they are what you would have said
     had you been bribed (by Wagner,
say) to defend yourself. Instead you merely

     changed wigs and smiled, satisfied
to speak by means of some brief exhalation,
     much as a Mohammedan

might spit, and by writing more tiny pieces
     with your left hand (though *for* both);
as if to inquire, by that very restraint

     of ecstasy which makes all
leisure possible—no instigator now,
     merely an institution—

"Where is the life that is not a new defeat?
     Yet where is the life that was
not always meant for a kind of victory?"

Richard Wagner

A disputed portrait by Nadar Jeune   *for Richard Burger*

No props—for once we have you unstaged, ideal
    genius at forty without
wadded-silk dressing-gown, wine-velvet beret,

    a villa filled with idols.
You stare off-camera at—what? Here at least
    there is more than meets the ear

cocked, this moment, for Frau Wesendonck's praises
    and for Cosima's prayers—
so much more ardent, at sixteen, than Minna's:

    a few infidelities
will bring far less sorrow than the long-drawn-out
    disloyalty of desire.

What we see is what we dream you must have been,
    boldly readying yourself
for what Baudelaire called the greatest honor

    a poet can have: to do
no more and no less than what he intended.
    Until your will had been done,

the difference between sanity and hysteria,
    illusion and reality,
had always been a matter of time: what was

    real, what was sane, had always
lasted longer—only truth was continuous.
    You would alter that, transform

our fears and even our fatigue, you would force
    time to change shape and by cold
legerdemain, from Ortrud to Klingsor, make

    event, mere happening, into
duration, having discovered the center
    of our every appetite

is in its metamorphoses. Wait, though—dates
    conflict, the size of the plate
is wrong, and you hated Nadar; for a man

    just over five feet, could these
long shanks be yours? Experts shrug, and we are left
    with the old dissatisfactions:

complete understanding of a dream includes
    the knowledge that it is one,
and such knowledge wakes us up. This is not you.

Charles Baudelaire

You were the hero inherent in Eros—
    "builder of cities" all right
but saboteur as well—wherefore you despised

    such indispensable prey
as readers who failed, despite your example,
    to pluck themselves a garden

from the garbage of the past. If we look hard
    at things they seem to look back;
out of a writhing greatcoat you stare at us

    with that splendid impatience
which is the deepest French virtue, "taken"
    by your lifelong friend between

hyperboles—at one extreme lilac gloves
    and black curls to your collar,
at the other Jeanne's insulted beauty and

    bald paralysis—but here
implacable, holding fast to a passion
    for exactitude. Today

you published ten poems you wanted to call
    Lesbiennes until advised
by Hyppolite Babou to name them *Fleurs du Mal* . . .

    Why not? you are so busy
with your current Poe translations and puzzled
    by favors to be curried

from George Sand, "poor dear dreadful little lady,
  always having a crow to pick
with Jean-Jacques!" You look at things, though, look until

   you don't know if they are you
or you they: it is the moment when what was
  ruin becomes a model,

Paris a synonym for both. Arbiter
  of ennui, you rummage on:
Mexican idols, a gilded Buddha, rag dolls

   might as well be our true God,
offensive concretion of the temporal
  process. We cannot erect

the New Jerusalem until we destroy
  Babylon; what do we use
in the building, you asked, but the same damned stones?

Edmond and Jules De Goncourt

Fiction was no help, though folly more than fact
     was what you found diverting
and made more than that for us—made it something

     halfway between dirty and
divagation, incidentally making
     yourselves, into the bargain,

masters of a vipers' nest coiled underneath
     every page, masquerading
as footnotes. Fancy discovering you both

     so handsome here, yet for once
indistinct—the blur is surely not Nadar's
     but some morose confusion

of your own—say the confession of "two lives
     never parted in labor
or in pleasure," knee to knee, white hands guarding

     cavernous crotches. Of course
one of you went first (syphilis at forty: so
     you must have been parted once

in pleasure), while the other just went on
     with the *Journal*, year by year . . .
Writing together, your task has been shedding

     one kind of glory to take
up another, yet it was child's play to you,
     and you took a child's delight

in it, pouring vinegar on troubled waters
    with a sort of awed contempt
while, during the dark discipline of Paris days,

    all your bibelots rattled
in the Rue Saint-Georges each time Baron Haussmann's
    wreckers struck again. Meanwhile

you needed nothing but each other; well, you had
    each other——no one reads you
now, and no wonder: a man writes to say *I*

    am not the only one, and
you were two. Then Jules died, and you, no longer
    "raising your eyelids as if

taking off your clothes," in Gautier's words, you,
    Edmond, sat down again to write . . .
Come dust now, come shadows, for the world is dead.

Gustave Doré

This is your last thin moment. Work fed you well,
    wealth followed and fondled—no
wonder the Goncourts mocked your pink face, "the full

    moon in a magic lantern."
England, at least, could be persuaded to switch
    the lantern on: Biblical

landscapes the Salon regularly refused,
    huge leathern daubs, sold out
in the London shop you bought to show them in.

    And all the rest, save Maman,
was a cheat—smart young men who aped your mufflers
    and marvelled at the magic

would not withstand your ardors. As if something
    was out of scale. . . . How the size
of things disappoints (your Ancient Mariner,

    even your Wandering Jew
were tiny tempests in the vast black teapots
    you brewed them in), not because

they are so small but because the mind itself
    is so huge. The engravings
persisted at a heat so white it would melt

    the very heart in your mouth.
Soon you had illustrated two hundred books,
    and no one came to dinner;

Gustave Doré

Maman was dead; the ink dried in its well;
    your Strasbourg was German now . . .
And at fifty, having prevailed on the world

    to see its classics your way,
you blew up, eclipsed by your own garish luck.
    You swallowed too much, even

the one boy who stayed (for brandy, you pleaded):
    le gigolo malgré lui . . .
When nothing was left to eat you had to die:

    as long as some reality
remains outside us, we are still alive
    come hell or high water, both

of which came with remarkable frequency
    until fire was just fussy
and the flood frivolous. Then the page went blank.

Théophile Gautier

My God, you're my age and look at you: a wreck!
    Lank across the "ruined brow"
and rippling to the ripely crusted collar,

    rusty locks to which no nose
but yours has the key—your cheeks furrow away
    from it as though from a prow

till the rancid wake of your beard rusts out in
    the shallows. You have been had
feature by feature, all fine once, all foul now,

    till only your eyes, sandbagged
against what overflow? stare from the leavings
    of wine, women and hashish.

What are you wearing? White leather, it looks like,
    a gown from Turkey, throttled
with a scarf, below the scurf, from Liberty . . .

    When the divine beds become
mortal battlefields, this flesh is the result:
    you had no need of heaven

or of hell either, but lived instead on chaos,
    reminding us *improper*
was first used of humans in your 1850's. . . .

    I guess I love you even so,
for beyond the national satisfactions
    of the mouth, beyond in fact

the daily business of revelation, you
  symbolize the paradox
assaulting us when we learn that history

  is merely experience.
Your hands are not seen—they shake too much to show—
  but it is a prejudice

to suppose instability must be sad
  or trivial; only those
who can still love their faults make good confessions,

  and yours are good as the Devil,
who is always the other thing than God, God
  gone to the Devil. No, not love,

it is envy I feel, contemplating you,
  your fate consumed by sacred
couplings in a burning world—consummated.

George Sand

You were comrades, *compères*, Nadar had even
    named a balloon after you,
so when, that afternoon in his studio—

    though you were sixty, beyond
seduction or at least beyond seducing,
    irreproachably chaptered

at Nohant in a rustle of no more than
    imaginary copulation—
when he asked you to sit for him as Racine

    you went along with the gag,
if it was one, wrapped yourself in red velvet
    and a Louis-something wig

left around for fancy-dress parties, and lo!
    disclose yourself a classic
in precisely the moral drag you managed

    to forego for a lifetime
of thriving on what others call intuition,
    though it is in fact no more

than a subtle human power of noticing,
    or attention, or simply
trust in experience. Neither the *grande dame*

    your dreadful novels flouted
nor the *grande amoureuse* you flattered yourself
    your lovers were not up to,

you still belong with the subversive poet
  you take off or put on here,
for you have discovered that to make choices

  is nothing, to take them less—
to create choices is everything. The ones
  you created were a trap

Racinian enough for your disguise: releasing
  inhibitions is quite as
compulsive, repetitive, and hysterical

  an operation (and opus)
as repressing them. Perhaps a genius
  though never a gentleman,

you pose with a flamboyant frumpishness past
  the dull coquetries of sex,
serenely heretical, efficient, real.

Nadar

A portrait by Nadar Jeune   *for Rosalind Krauss*

You will be obscured by a cloud of postures
    and a roster of great names,
but here, in your high thirties, you can hardly

    be more distinct, distinguished
by hair, hope and the heroic resolution
    to present life with an image

unretouched—had it not been the fallacy
    of centuries to *correct?*
Edited, glossed, conflated, expurgated—

    what was left to believe in?
All men are mad when they are alone, almost
    all women: that was your text

and your testimony, the acknowledgment
    of a balloonist whose pride
it was to announce that countless things have been

    seen and remain to be seen,
and for whom humility was equivalent
    to seeing things as they are,

opacity being a great discoverer.
    Why else is it your portraits
loom likelier for us now than all preening

    identifications since?
Because you made your Act between consenting
    adults a Sacred Game

55

wherein the dead god is recognized, the change
  being from darkness to light
and revelation—the god reborn. You were

  our demiurge: from a world
where chaos and cosmos are superimposed,
  from a world where anything

can happen but nothing happens twice, you spoke
  your *fiat lux* or *fiat*
nox to bring forth the creation of nature

  against nature within nature.
Now you have sixty years in which to retrieve
  the visionary from the visual,

then fade into the once and future classics,
  leaving us to enlarge on
what cannot be divided, individuals.

(III)

Domesticities

We ate from the dish of eyes
and as eyes met, making out
light by darkness, we hungered:
>   the dish is a questioning of the dish.

We drank from the cup of hands
and as hands met, reaching down
for what was up, we thirsted:
>   the cup is a questioning of the cup.

We slept in the bed of flesh
and as flesh met, melting back
to the lost action, we kept
>   forgiving, and for good: no questions asked.

Another Invitation

Lord, they sound *triste*, my first love poems,
    whose frank Midwestern totems
        all bear French titles—
as if Baudelaire could help me out
    of Cleveland! *L'invitation*
        au voyage turned down
or inside out, certainly, by each
    dim lover, those bright strangers
        reluctant to come:
Pig-iron boats were leaving for the lake
    (Lake Erie), *slowly the loud*
        bridges had risen
(drawn across the sick Cuyahoga);
    "*A landscape for the lonely*
        or the lewd," *you said,*
the river sighed in its bed, and when
    gulls were harsh in their abuse
        you did not look up—
I remember how your face went blind . . .
    Enough of that. I decamped
        within two decades,
not to make the scene but to adore
    the scenery of Elsewhere,
        and I write from there.

Here is a lake too, of course, the waves
    rendered by Pietro's brush—
        or Ambrogio's,
they were brothers, they died in the same
    plague year, 1348:
        i Lorenzetti—

the waves resolved in green pulsations
    to resemble a sea of grass;
        but let me conflate
their two little images, which are
    all I have (though sufficient)
        to prove my Elsewhere
seductive. On a pair of panels,
    first this crystalline city
        with three oaks, two ships
offshore, and no human soul to blur
    the interval of windows,
        walls, towers, and look!
in the right corner, a drawbridge too,
    leading down from Siena's
        Public Palace, or
one very much like it. . . . And then this
    harbor underneath a bare
        hillside, three more oaks,

and the spotty fields beyond—I know
    it is a harbor down there
        because of the reeds,
five to a clump, at the water's edge
    and because of a boat
        safe in the shallows—
moored for now, that boat, but as certain
    to depart as if its name
        read *Cytherea*
on the bow curved crisp as an ear or
    curved slack as a sexual
        organ: a black boat
on a pale shore, and no one in sight.
    No one has ever been here
        (unless you will come),

yet people are not what is absent,
 not us, not the animals—
  something is missing . . .
One thing to notice in these landscapes—
 transparent, sane as only
  Elsewhere can be—
is that there is no horizon, no sky,
 and nothing stands against
  heaven, dark or light.

Come with me, love, neither dim nor bright
 but as you are, seen as these
  things—a green tower
beside a red one, edges of things—
 give us themselves: without God,
  unable to mean
more than they appear, just eternal,
 just ordinary. Come, love,
  let us be fellow
travellers: the boat rides on no more
 than water, the drawbridge drops
  to merely land. Come,
you see? God is out of the picture,
 not as if He had been done
  in by other gods
of greater power—simply that He
 came to nothing, leaving no
  text, no throne, no soul
in the soil, as if He had never
 inhabited earth. No more
  terrible portents,
love, no dread meanings if you come, but
 this castle, that lake, the light . . .
  Maybe we shall go.

Codes

in the record sleeve of a Mozart opera

By now I have your face by heart,
I have your voice by ear; I know
from quavers between glass and hand
as you pour the Amarone
that there is a parallel qualm
whether we will make love tonight;
and from our laughter when I say
"this wine is over the hill" and
you—we are in Rome—reply "yes,
love, the Palatine," that we will.

A universe is coaxed into
Being by such analogies,
seven Planets with seven Ores
they must engender underground—
similitudes, signs I would take
gladly for wonders: what is marked
can be remarked, what remembered
dismembered. But just envisage
news that is subtler, signatures
of the self beyond all telling . . .

How am I to have *them*, by what
organ of apprehension, more
cordially tuned than heart and ear,
have the tiny repeating alps
of your cardiogram, say, make
sense when none of the senses can?
These languages lie around us,
tapeworms to starve out meaning from

the mind, that last Laocoön,
festooned in miles of alpha-waves—

interminable lilac scriptures
according to Marjerrison,
Moruzzi, Magoun, Mulholland,
Matović and Mundy-Castle:
what matters, finally? is mind
matter? After such processing,
what can six gray eminences
tell me? "Not much, Richard. Maybe
the waves account for something wrong—
maybe they're what haloes come from."

Movements, changes, electrical
energies "discharged"—so many
hieroglyphs on the graph: we can
conceive ourselves only so far
as we can repeat ourselves, and
the needles waver on, stupid
aureoles, "something wrong," no more
than one narrow disease of things
that are. Yet I have learned to read
some semaphors of your semblance

(only the wound speaks its own word),
and I am patient with the great
silence where we are vulnerable
—do not think me a tragic figure—
or where we are invulnerable,
which is worse. Around us, I say,
these languages lie: consider
the shells we collect on the beach,
encoded surely with the sonnet
sequence conchs indite to the tide,

if only we could translate: *once*
upon a time I lived happily
ever after. Consider furthermore
what patience has already done
for us (are we done for?) in this
recording: lines of force (I speak
in the vocabulary of Rome
we must learn to use when we are
creatures of time) whirling beneath
an adamant needle, this time,

and *heard!* the tremulous spiral
comes out *La Clemenza di Tito*,
labyrinthine labors to bring forth
open secrets and the ringing
dark. It is a kind of pledge, love:
the disc revolves, our laughter gives
a signal for self-possession.
Wait. Devise. Divine. There is
nothing worth doing that does not
have to be done again. Listen . . .

With the Remover to Remove

Not that he wanted nothing to change—
the noon sun shadowless and the moon
nailed fast between the slow Dippers—not

that he expected it all to stay
as it was when he had first found out
the difference between a false dawn

and a false dusk; but it was too much:
the Spring, returning, made scandalous
demands, and who could meet each Christmas

with sufficient cheer to justify
the challenge of yet one more New Year?
His love affairs, as well, had altered

past enduring—did not the last one
burn itself out to a small cinder
in next to no time? Children of friends

were older now than boys he met in bars
where he no longer met friends, of course,
but erratic and beautiful freaks—

perhaps they were the children of friends.
Yes, it was too much, or too little
of which he made too much of late . . . Late!

Imagine calling New York City,
where nothing succeeded like excess
and nothing else succeeded at all,

a product of the Temperate Zone!
He must leave it, he *would* leave to have
something left to himself: the leavings

of the City's life immured him now—
another month of metamorphosis
would move him to an immolation

in his own apartment, pyre and all!
With April huffing and puffing hard
on his heels, he booked passage and took

a few impassive books to keep himself
in countenance among the tropical
facelessness (what else, he conjectured,

had constituted the fabled Lure
of the Tropics?)—the boat was terror,
the books no help, the crew's tanned faces

far too distinct. Already he longed
to stop the soft machine of ocean,
switch the damn thing off, make it go dead.

But it went on, and on, and onward
thereupon, delivering him up,
more alive than so much *mal-de-mer*

could possibly warrant or excuse,
to an island which appeared to be
all edges: whatever he surveyed

(feeling remarkably better now)
something seemed to be held toward him
out of the surf which so soundly cuffed

the beach and its smart blue sleeve beyond.
It was a promise from the sea that came
to him as the project of a mask,

an air-pipe, and black rubber flippers—
a promise or at least a premise
that down there, just beneath the surface,

lay release from the variorum
of perspectives which so obsessed him.
He put them on, panicked a little

at first, but soon (the flippers aiding
immeasurably—there was no need
to wriggle so) was in his element.

Inches away, under his wide eyes,
lay another world: soundless but for
the reassuring repetition

of his own breath that came and went back
for more where that came from; seemingly
aimless, though some of the blue flashes

pretending to be fish made him doubt
these presentiments of apathy;
and changeless—that was what moved him most

about the vision moving still, still
so unmoved. The purple tentacles,
stirred by a rhythm which seemed to be

that of his own respiration, reached
for nothing but themselves, the green fans
rotated majestically, filled

and voided by some inexpressible
nobility of impulse in which
ugliness describes itself, beauty

is merely uttered. Nothing would change,
even the pattern of erratic
and beautiful freaks (where had he heard

such a phrase?) languidly pursuing
or pursued across the brain-corals,
undeterred by the gorgeous tumors

of black sea-urchins patient in wait
for victims as indispensable
as they were unimaginable.

Dissolving views! This undersea life
was not intended but intense, too
lovely to rise to penance or regret,

and too lovely to sink to revenge.
Everything was known as something else—
parrot-fish, eel-grass, those brain-corals—

nature was unavailable save
to the old names, it was merely there,
intrinsically elegiac,

like his own body, magically
hung above the wavering marine,
its weightless shadow without menace

to the singular societies
which moved about their being unscathed
by the huge observer overhead—

moved, he was sure of it it now, in time
to his own echoing lungs: in fact
was it not his breath by which *they* breathed?

Were they not, devil-fish, angel-fish
and all the rest, the contents of one
infinite, eternal body—his?

Having guessed this, he could go; having
pondered by such irresponsible
levitation the pure likelihood

of outweighing the sea, he could get
back to his prose and that progress where
the pain is remembered; having seen,

there would be no longer any need
to secede. So he might recover
the great city, which is where we are

most vulnerable, and times to come
find him smiling at even younger
faces of boys he barely knew, though

patient with their mortality and
his own not-to-be-helped completion
as he stroked, with an odd significance,

a talismanic stalk of coral,
apparently unvexed by the turn
and turn about of the latest screw.

It had happened down there; between them,
the sea and the mask had permitted
the vision he surfaced from shivering

a little, but with knowledge, not fear,
saying: *I am not I, now that I see.*
Nothing changes, it is I that change.

With a Potpourri from Down Under

Anything but rotten, such flowers are ill
named, remaining exempt from the compost fate
by a decorum of fatigue, keeping still
the power to generate
a world of their own, long since over the hill,

or of ours. Inhale them and you can recall
—what? Whatever is recoverable just
and only just for having been, after all,
forgotten. Closer—you must
put your nose right into the powdery ball

of bloom to get the good of it, past the blue
of unrecognizable gentians, past wild
roses tamed to mild rose, even past a few
patently dead leaves reconciled
by dust with the livid petals. There. Now you

have it, strong for all the insistent pastels
(as if life were forged by Marie Laurencin—
or death, for that matter), now you have the smells
of a room we first met in:
two kittens, pot and the pungence that wells

up out of the ampoules of amyl nitrite
apparently used, *chez* Tom, instead of *sauce
béchamel*. That was a forgone appetite,
though it makes less of a loss
if you couple the lovemaking our first night

with a myth instead of with a person——me,
yourself, whoever in between: we become
    creators when we have a past. So make free
      with the odors coming from
this irresponsible present: breathe deeply,

    and a bed in Vermont will be unmade; stir
the wan remains and you will have invented
    closets in Florence which were
      identically scented,
clearings in Hawaii heretofore a blur——

    I know. I've tried it, slipping habit's traces
by a quick whiff myself, gaining from partial
    immersion the totally risen graces
      of going down into all
the intimate reek, the must of dark places.

    Now you take over. Each garden is a grave,
I grant you, but there are resurrections here:
    our senses make us giants in what time we have
      (Proust's law)——use yours then, my dear,
on a gift that savors of more than we can save.

Richard Howard

*Richard Howard was born in 1929 in Cleveland,
Ohio, and studied at Columbia University and the
Sorbonne. He is a distinguished translator from the
French and a critic of great versatility. His six
earlier books of poems are* QUANTITIES (*1962*),
THE DAMAGES (*1967*), UNTITLED SUBJECTS
(*1969*), FINDINGS (*1971*), TWO-PART INVEN-
TIONS (*1974*) *and* FELLOW FEELINGS (*1976*).
He is the author of ALONE WITH AMERICA: Essays
on the Art of Poetry in the United States since 1950,
and of the commentary in PREFERENCES, *a critical
anthology of the relations between fifty-one
contemporary poets and the poetry of the past.*